ACCOUNTING LIFEPA
BUSINESS SIMULAT

CONTENTS

BUSINESS SIMULATION FOR LARSON'S TOURS

Author: Daniel L. Ritzman, B.S.
Editors: Alan Christopherson, M.S.
                   Jennifer L. Davis, B.S.

ALPHA OMEGA
PUBLICATIONS

300 North McKemy Avenue, Chandler, Arizona 85226-2618

ACCOUNTING LIFEPAC 10
BUSINESS SIMULATION

2.5 pgs per day
no new
vocab!

OVERVIEW

This LIFEPAC will review all the accounting procedures learned in LIFEPACs 1 through 9 by using a business simulation. This simulation incorporates all the steps used to complete an accounting cycle. The business in this simulation uses a journal and general ledger to summarize all transactions.

OBJECTIVES

When you have completed this LIFEPAC you will be able to complete the following accounting procedures:

1. Open the general ledger accounts.

2. Record transactions in a journal.

3. Prepare a payroll register.

4. Prepare an employer payroll tax expense summary and record the entry for payroll taxes expense.

5. Post journal transactions to the general ledger.

6. Prepare a trial balance on the worksheet.

7. Record the adjusting entries on the worksheet.

8. Calculate net income/net loss to complete the worksheet.

9. Prepare the following financial statements:

    a. Income Statement

    b. Statement of Owner's Equity

    c. Balance Sheet

10. Record and post the adjusting entries.

11. Record and post the closing entries.

12. Prepare a post-closing trial balance.

BUSINESS SIMULATION FOR LARSON'S TOURS

Introduction to Larson's Tours

Larson's Tours, owned by Olive Larson, is a service business organized as a sole proprietorship. Larson's Tours organizes tours for individuals or groups. Mrs. Larson rents office space at a local mall. She has hired employees for the office. All other services needed by the business are subcontracted for each individual tour or vacation. The business derives its revenue from tour fees.

Fiscal Period. Larson's Tours uses a one-month accounting cycle or fiscal period. The fiscal period begins on March 1 and ends on March 31 of the current year.

Payroll. Larson's Tours is required by federal law to withhold federal income tax, FICA tax, and Medicare tax from each employee's wages. The business is also subject to payroll taxes at the following rates: FICA, 6.2%; Medicare, 1.45%; federal unemployment, 0.8%; state unemployment, 4.3% (NOTE: This is a different rate than used in previous LIFEPACs. Rates will vary from state to state).

Employee Information. Employee information for the two payrolls in March is shown below:

March 15th payroll: Empl. #1 – Andrea Baker, Single, 1 Allowance, Gross Pay $800.00
                                Empl. #2 – Sommer Craig, Single, 1 Allowance, Gross Pay $800.00

March 31st payroll: Empl. #1 – Andrea Baker, Single, 1 Allowance, Gross Pay $800.00
                                Empl. #2 – Sommer Craig, Single, 1 Allowance, Gross Pay $800.00
                                Empl. #3 – Season Lewis, Single, 0 Allowance, Gross Pay $200.00

Chart of Accounts

Open the general ledger, using the following chart of accounts:

Larson's Tours Chart of Accounts General Ledger	
(100) ASSETS	**(400) REVENUE**
110 Cash *(requires two ledger pages)*	410 Tour Fees
120 Petty Cash	**(500) EXPENSES**
130 Supplies	510 Advertising Expense
140 Prepaid Insurance	520 Automobile Expense
150 Automobile	530 Insurance Expense
160 Office Equipment	540 Miscellaneous Expense:
(200) LIABILITIES	Postage, bank charges, lunches, equipment repair, office cleaning, credit card charges
210 A to Z Office Supply	550 Payroll Taxes Expense
220 Employee Income Tax Payable	560 Rent Expense
230 FICA Tax Payable	570 Salary Expense
240 First City Bank	580 Supplies Expense
250 Medicare Tax Payable	590 Utilities Expense
260 Unemployment Tax Payable–Federal	
270 Unemployment Tax Payable–State	
(300) OWNER'S EQUITY	
310 Olive Larson, Capital	
320 Olive Larson, Drawing	
330 Income Summary	

Source Documents

The following is a description of the various source documents, their abbreviations and the transactions for which they are used in this business simulation.

Document	Abbreviation	Transactions
Register Tapes	T	Cash and credit card receipts from tour fees
Receipts	R	Cash received from sources other than tour fees
Check Stubs	Ck	Cash payments
Memorandum	M	Transactions directed by bookkeeper, accountant or owner

4

Date 2003		Account Title and Explanation	Doc No.	Post. Ref.	General Debit		General Credit	
MARCH	1	Cash		110	22,000	00		
		Olive Larson, Capital	R1	310			22,000	00
	2	OFFICE EQUIPMENT		160	1500	00		
		Olive Larson, Capital	M1	310			1500	00
	3	Automobile		150	17,950	00		
		Cash		110			7800	00
		FIRST CITY BANK	CK101	240			10,150	00
	4	Supplies		130	1800	00		
		Cash	CK102	110			1800	00
	4	RENT EXPENSE		560	1250	00		
		Cash	CK103	110			1250	00
	4	MiscellANEOUS EXPENSE		540	6. 0	80		
		Cash	CK104	110			6. 0	80
	4	Cash		110	2,675	00		
		TOUR FEES	T4	410			2675	00
	6	Prepaid INSURANCE		140	3,280	00		
		Cash	CK105	110			3,280	00
	6	Supplies		130	895	00		
		A + o Z OFFICE Supply	M2	210			895	00
	7	Utilities EXPENSE		580	235	00		
		Cash	CK106	110			235	00
	7	Automobile Expense		520	17	90		
		Cash	CK107	110			17	90
	8	Miscellaneous EXPENSE		540	98	00		
		Cash	CK108	110			98	00
	9	Automobile Expense		520	495	00		
		Cash	CK109	110			495	00
	9	Olive Larson, Drawing		320	850	00		
		Cash	CK110	110			850	00
	10	A to Z OFFICE Supply		210	450	00		
		Cash	CK111	110			450	00

Date 2003		Account Title and Explanation	Doc No.	Post. Ref.	General Debit		General Credit	
March	10	Utilities Expense		590	790	00		
		Cash	Ck112	110			790	00
	11	Cash		110	7,690	00		
		Tour Fees	T11	410			7690	00
	13	Miscellaneous Expense		540	108	00		
		Cash	Ck113	110			108	00
	13	Advertisement Expense		510	975	00		
		Cash	Ck114	110			975	00
	13	Miscellaneous Expense		510	110	00		
		Cash	Ck115	110			110	00
	13	Automobile Expense		520	23	00		
		Cash	Ck116	110			23	00
	14	Advertising Expense		510	83	50		
		Cash	Ck117	110			83	50
	14	A to Z Office Supply		210	445	00		
		Cash	Ck118	110			445	00
	15	Supplies Expense		580	695	00		
		A to Z Office Supply	M3	210			695	00
	15	Salary Expense		570	1600	00		
		Employee Tax Payable		220			174	00
		FICA Tax Payable		230			99	20
		Medicare Payable		250			23	20
		Cash	Ck119	110			1303	60
	15	Payroll Tax Expense		550	204	00		
		FICA Tax Payable		230			99	20
		Medicare Payable		250			23	20
		Unemploy. Tax Payable Federal		260			12	80
		Unemploy. Tax Payable State	M5	270			68	80
	16	Miscellaneous Expense		540	19	80		
		Cash	Ck120	110			19	80
	16	First City Bank		240	350	00		
		Cash	Ck121	110			350	00

Date	Account Title and Explanation	Doc No.	Post. Ref.	General Debit		General Credit	
March 17	Miscellaneous		540	87	90		
	Cash	CK122	110			87	90
17	Prepaid Insurance		140	1860	00		
	Cash	CK123	110			1860	00
18	Olive Larison, Drawing		320	850	00		
	Cash	CK124	110			850	00
18	Automobile Expense		520	79	95		
	Cash	CK125	110			79	95
18	Cash		110	5670	00		
	Tour Fees	T18	410			5670	00
18	Miscellaneous Expense		540	158	00		
	Cash	CK126	110			158	00
20	Utilities		590	367	00		
	Cash	CK127	110			367	00
20	Miscellaneous Expense		540	110	00		
	Cash	CK128	110			110	00
21	Automobile Expense		520	82	50		
	Cash	CK129	110			82	50
21	A to Z Office Supply		210	250	00		
	Cash	CK130	110			250	00
22	Office Equipment		160	1,195	00		
	Cash	CK131	110			1,195	00
23	Advertising Expense		510	60	00		
	Cash	CK132	110			60	00
23	Miscellaneous Expense		540	7	50		
	Cash	CK133	110			7	50
24	Supplies		120	295	00		
	Cash	CK134	110			295	00
25	Cash		110	3,895	00		
	Tours Fees	T25	410			3895	00
27	Miscellaneous Expense		540	318	00		
	Cash	CK135	110			318	00

206.40

JOURNAL

Date 2001	Account Title and Explanation	Doc No.	Post. Ref.	General Debit		General Credit	
March 28	Automobile Expense		520	27	00		
	Cash	CK136	110			27	00
30	Oliver Larson, Drawing		320	850	00		
	Cash	CK137	110			850	00
30	Miscellaneous Expense		540	9	75		
	Cash	M9	110			9	75
30	Cash		110	1975	00		
	Tours Fees	T31	410			1975	00
30	Petty Cash		120	300	00		
	Cash	CK138	110			300	00
30	Miscellaneous Expense		540	682	00		
	Cash	M10	110			680	00
31	Salary Expense		570	1800	00		
	Employee Income Tax Payable		220			188	00
	FICA Tax Payable		230			111	60
	Medicare Tax Payable		250			26	10
	Cash	CK139	110			1474	30
31	Payroll Tax Expense		550	229	50		
	FICA Tax Payable		230			111	60
	Medicare Tax Payable		250			26	10
	Unempl. Tax Payable-Fed		260			14	40
	Unempl. Tax Payable-State	M12	270			77	40

Date 2003		Account Title and Explanation	Doc No.	Post. Ref.	General Debit		General Credit	
		Adjusting Entries						
March	31	Supply Expense		580	2505	00		
		Supplies		130			2505	00
	31	Insurance Expense		530	3110	00		
		Prepaid Insurance		140			3110	00
		Closing Entries						
March	31	Tour Frees (Sales)		410	21905	00		
		Income Summary		330			21905	00
	31	Income Summary		330	15650	10		
		Advertising Expense		510			1118	50
		Automobile "		520			725	35
		Insurance "		530			3110	00
		Miscellaneous "		540			1715	75
		Payroll Taxes "		550			433	50
		Rent "		560			1250	00
		Salary "		570			3400	00
		Supplies "		580			2505	00
		Utilities "		590			1392	00
	31	Income Summary		330	6254	90		
		Olive Larson, Capital		310			6254	90
	31	Olive Larson, Capital		310	2550	00		
		Olive Larson, Drawing		320			2550	00

11.60
11.60
$223.20

21905
15650
62549°

Account Title: Cash   **Account No.** 110

Date	Explanation	Post. Ref.	Debit		Credit		Balance Debit		Balance Credit	
2003										
March 1		J1	2200	00			22000	00		
3		J1			7800	00	14200	00	14200	0
4		J1			1800	00	12400	00	1400	
4		J1			1250	00	11150	06	11150	00
4		J1			6	80	11143	20	11143	20
4		J1	2675	00			13818	20		
6		J1			3280	00	10,538	20	10,538	20
7		J1			235	00	10,303	20	10,303	20
7		J1			17	90	10,285	30	10,285	30
8		J1			98	00	10,187	30	10,187	30
9		J1			495	00	9,692	30	9,692	30
9		J1			850	00	8,842	30	8,842	30
10		J1			450	00	8,392	30	8392	30
10		J2			790	00	7602	30	7602	30
11		J2	7,690	00			15,292	30		
13		J2			108	00	15184	30	15184	30
13		J2			975	00	14209	30	14209	30
13		J2			110	00	14099	30	14099	30
13		J2			23	00	14076	30	14076	30
14		J2			83	50	13992	80	13992	80
14		J2			445	00	13547	80	13547	80
15		J2			1303	60	12244	20	12244	20
16		J2			19	80	12224	40	12224	40
16		J2			350	00	11874	40	11874	40
17		J3			87	90	11786	50	11786	50
17		J3			1860	00	9926	50	9926	50
18		J3			850	00	9076	50	9076	50
18		J3			79	95	8996	55	8996	55
18		J3	5670	00			14666	65		
18		J3			158	00	14508	55	14508	65
20		J3			367	00	14141	55	14141	55
20					110	00	14031	55	14031	55

Account Title: Petty Cash   **Account No.** 110

Date 2003		Explanation	Post. Ref.	Debit		Credit		Balance Debit		Credit	
March	21		J3			82	50	13949	05		
	21		J3			250	00	13699	05		
	22		J3			1195	00	12504	05		
	23		J3			60	00	12444	05		
	23		J3			7	50	12436	55		
	24		J3			295	00	12141	55		
	25		J3	3895	00			16,036	55		
	27		J3			318	00	15,718	55		
	28		J4			27	00	15,691	55		
	30		J4			850	00	14,841	55		
	30		J4			9	75	14,831	80		
	30		J4	1975	00			16806	80		
	30		J4			300	00	16506	80		
	30		J4			682	00	15824	80		
	31		J4			1474	30	14350	50		

Account Title: Petty Cash   **Account No.** 120

Date 2003		Explanation	Post. Ref.	Debit		Credit		Balance Debit		Credit	
March	30		J4	300	00			300	00		

13

Account Title: Supplies — Account No. 130

Date 2003		Explanation	Post. Ref.	Debit		Credit		Balance Debit		Balance Credit	
March	4		J1	1800	00			1800	00		
	6		J1	895	00			2695	00		
	15		J2	695	00			3390	00		
	24		J3	295	00			3685	00		
	31		J5			2505	00	1180	00		

Account Title: Prepaid Insurance — Account No. 140

Date 2003		Explanation	Post. Ref.	Debit		Credit		Balance Debit		Balance Credit	
March	6		J1	3280	00			3280	00		
	17		J3	1860	00			5140	00		
	31		J5			3110	00			2030	00

Account Title: Automobile — Account No. 150

Date 2003		Explanation	Post. Ref.	Debit		Credit		Balance Debit		Balance Credit	
March	3		J1	1795	00			1795	00		

Account Title: Office Equipment   **Account No.** 160

Date 2003	Explanation	Post. Ref.	Debit		Credit		Balance Debit		Balance Credit	
March 2		J1	1500	00			1500	00		
22		J3	1195	00			2695	00		

Account Title: A to Z Office Supply   **Account No.** 210

Date 2003	Explanation	Post. Ref.	Debit		Credit		Balance Debit		Balance Credit	
March 6		J1			895	00			895	00
10		J1	450	00					445	00
14		J2	445	00					—	
21		J2			695	00			695	00
21		J3	250	00					445	00

Account Title: Employee Income Tax Payable   **Account No.** 220

Date 2003	Explanation	Post. Ref.	Debit		Credit		Balance Debit		Balance Credit	
March 15		J2			174	00			174	00
		J4			188	00			362	00

Account Title: FICA Tax Payable   Account No. 230

Date 2003		Explanation	Post. Ref.	Debit		Credit		Balance Debit		Balance Credit	
March	15		J2			99	20			99	20
	15		J2			99	20			198	40
	31		J4			111	60			310	00
	31		J4			111	60			421	60

Account Title: First City Bank   Account No. 240

Date 2003		Explanation	Post. Ref.	Debit		Credit		Balance Debit		Balance Credit	
March	3		J1			10,150	00			10,150	00
	16		J2	350	00					9 800	00

Account Title: Medicare Tax Payable   Account No. 250

Date 2003		Explanation	Post. Ref.	Debit		Credit		Balance Debit		Balance Credit	
March	15		J2			23	20				
	15		J2			23	20			46	40
	31		J4			26	10			72	50
	31		J4			26	10			98	60

ACCOUNTING

ten

LIFEPAC TEST

72 / 90

Name_____

Date_____

Score_____

58%

LIFEPAC TEST ACCOUNTING 10

Answer the following questions by referring to the appropriate section of this LIFEPAC (each answer, 3 points).

PART I – JOURNAL

Answers:

1. What is the amount charged to First City Bank on March 3rd? 1. $10,150.00

2. What is the amount of prepaid insurance purchased on March 6th? 2. $3,280.00

3. What is the total amount of Tour Fees on March 11th? 3. $7,690.00

4. What credit amount on March 15th equals Net Pay? 4. $1303.60

5. What is the amount paid to A to Z Office Supply on March 14th? 5. $445.00

6. What is the total Payroll Taxes Expense on March 31st? 6. $204.00

PART II – GENERAL LEDGER

7. What is the balance of the Cash account on March 31st? 7. $14350.50

8. When was the Petty Cash account established? 8. March 30, 2003

9. What was the owner's original investment in the business? 9. $22,000.00

10. What is the balance of the Income Summary account after adjusting and closing entries are posted? 10. 0

11. What is the balance of the owner's Capital account before adjusting and closing entries are posted? 11. $23500.00

12. What is the balance of the Prepaid Insurance account after adjusting and closing entries are posted? 12. $2,030.00

PART III – PAYROLL REGISTER

13. What is the total payroll for March 15th? 13. $1600

14. What is the total deduction for Andrea Baker on the March 15th payroll? 14. $148.20

15. How many tax allowances are claimed by Sommer Craig? 15. 1

16. What is the total payroll for March 31st? 16. $1800

17. What is the total FICA Tax withheld for the March 31st payroll? 17. $111.60

18. What is the marital status of Season Lewis? 18. Single

1

Test Scores

Book 6   6

Quiz Test 1 - 95   Test 98

          2 - 98

          3 - 99
             ―――――
           97.3

Book - 7

Quizz 1 - ~~100~~ 97   Test 7 - 96 %

          2 - 100

          3 - 94
           ―――――
           97

Book - 8   Test 8 93 %

Quizz 1 - 100

       2 - 100

Quiz 3 - 93
          97.6

Book 9   Test 9   90 %

Quiz 1 - 100

       2 - 90

                    Test 10 - 88 %

       3 - 94   94.6

PART IV – WORK SHEET

Answers:

19. What is the Trial Balance debit total?

(19) $38,505.50

20. What is the Supplies Expense adjustment?

ask ?

20. $2505.00

21. What is the net income for Larson's Tours?

21. $6,254.90

22. What is the final total for the Balance Sheet credit column?

(22) $38,505.50

23. What is the total of the Adjustments credit column?

23. $5615

24. What is the total revenue received by Larson's Tours for the month of March?

24. $21,905.00

PART V – FINANCIAL STATEMENTS

25. What are the total assets on the Balance Sheet?

25. $38,505.50

26. What is the net increase in capital on the Statement of Owner's Equity?

26. $7754.90

27. What is the owner's capital on the Balance Sheet?

27. $27,204.90

28. What is the total of the credit column on the Post-Closing Trial Balance?

28. $38505.50

29. What are the total expenses on the Income Statement?

29. $15,650.10

30. What are the total liabilities on the Balance Sheet?

(30) $11,600.60

NOTES

Account Title: Unemployment Tax Payable - Federal   **Account No.** 260

Date	Explanation	Post. Ref.	Debit		Credit		Balance Debit		Balance Credit	
2003										
March 15		J2			12	80			12	80
31		J4			14	40			27	20

Account Title: Unemployment Tax Payable - State   **Account No.** 270

Date	Explanation	Post. Ref.	Debit		Credit		Balance Debit		Balance Credit	
2003										
March 15		J2			68	80			68	80
31		J4			77	40			146	20

Account Title: Olive Larson, Capital   **Account No.** 310

Date	Explanation	Post. Ref.	Debit		Credit		Balance Debit		Balance Credit	
2003										
March 1		J1			22,000	00			22000	00
2		J1			1500	00			23500	00

17

Account Title: Olive Larson, Drawing **Account No.** 320

Date 2003		Explanation	Post. Ref.	Debit		Credit		Balance Debit		Credit	
March	9		J1	850	00			850	00		
	18		J3	850	00			1700	00		
	30		J4	850	00			250	00		

Account Title: Income Summary **Account No.** 330

Date 2003		Explanation	Post. Ref.	Debit		Credit		Balance Debit		Credit	
March	31		J5			21905	00			21905	00
	31		J5	15650	10					6254	90
	31		J5	6254	90					—	

Account Title: Town Fees **Account No.** 410

Date 2003		Explanation	Post. Ref.	Debit		Credit		Balance Debit		Credit	
March	4		J1			2675	00			2675	00
	11		J2			7690	00			10,365	00
	18		J3			5670	00			16035	00
	25		J3			3895	00			19930	00
	30		J4			1975	00			21,905	00
	31		J5	21,905	00					—	

Account Title: Advertising Expense   **Account No.** 510

Date 2003		Explanation	Post. Ref.	Debit		Credit		Balance Debit		Balance Credit	
March	13		J2	975	00			975	00		
	14		J2	83	50			1058	50		
	23		J3	60	00			1118	50		
	31		J5			1118	50	—			

Account Title: Automobil Expense   **Account No.** 520

Date 2003		Explanation	Post. Ref.	Debit		Credit		Balance Debit		Balance Credit	
March	7		J1	17	90			17	90		
	9		J1	495	00			512	90		
	13		J2	23	00			535	90		
	18		J3	79	95			615	85		
	21		J3	82	50			698	35		
	28		J4	27	00			725	35		
	31		J5			725	35	—			

Account Title: Insurance Expense   **Account No.** 530

Date 2003		Explanation	Post. Ref.	Debit		Credit		Balance Debit		Balance Credit	
March	31		J5	3110	00	2675	00	3110	00	2675	00
	31		J5			3110	00	—			

Account Title: Miscellaneous Expense — Account No. 540

Date 2003		Explanation	Post. Ref.	Debit		Credit		Balance Debit		Balance Credit	
March	4		J1	6	80			6	80		
	8		J1	98	00			104	80		
	13		J2	108	00			212	80		
	13		J2	110	00			322	80		
	16		J2	19	80			342	60		
	17		J3	87	90			430	50		
	18		J3	158	00			588	50		
	20		J3	110	00			698	50		
	23		J3	7	50			706	00		
	27		J3	318	00			1024	00		
	30		J4	9	75			1033	75		
	30		J4	682	00			1715	75		
	31		J5			1715	75	—			

Account Title: Payroll Tax Expense — Account No. 550

Date 2003		Explanation	Post. Ref.	Debit		Credit		Balance Debit		Balance Credit	
March	15		J2	204	00			204	00		
	31		J4	229	50			433	50		
	31		J5			433	50	—			

Account Title: Rent Expense — Account No. 560

Date 2003		Explanation	Post. Ref.	Debit		Credit		Balance Debit		Balance Credit	
March	4		J1	1250	00			1250	00		
	31		J5			1250	00	—			

Account Title: Salary Expense   Account No. 570

Date 2003		Explanation	Post. Ref.	Debit		Credit		Balance Debit		Balance Credit	
March	15		J2	1600	00			1600	00		
	31		J4	1800	00			3400	00		
	31		J5			3400	00	—			

Account Title: Supplies Expense   Account No. 580

Date 2003		Explanation	Post. Ref.	Debit		Credit		Balance Debit		Balance Credit	
March	31		J5	2505	00			2505	00		
	31		J5			2505	00	—			

Account Title: Utilities Expense   Account No. 590

Date 2003		Explanation	Post. Ref.	Debit		Credit		Balance Debit		Balance Credit	
March	7		J1	235	00			235	00		
	10		J2	790	00			1025	00		
	20		J3	367	00			1392	00		
	31		J5			1392	00	—			

Federal Income Tax Withholding Table

SINGLE Persons- SEMIMONTHLY Payroll Period
(For Wages Paid in 2000)

If the wages are-		And the number of withholding allowances claimed is-										
At least	But less than	0	1	2	3	4	5	6	7	8	9	10
		The amount of income tax to be withheld is-										
$0	$115	0	0	0	0	0	0	0	0	0	0	0
115	120	1	0	0	0	0	0	0	0	0	0	0
120	125	2	0	0	0	0	0	0	0	0	0	0
125	130	3	0	0	0	0	0	0	0	0	0	0
130	135	3	0	0	0	0	0	0	0	0	0	0
135	140	4	0	0	0	0	0	0	0	0	0	0
140	145	5	0	0	0	0	0	0	0	0	0	0
145	150	6	0	0	0	0	0	0	0	0	0	0
150	155	6	0	0	0	0	0	0	0	0	0	0
155	160	7	0	0	0	0	0	0	0	0	0	0
160	165	8	0	0	0	0	0	0	0	0	0	0
165	170	9	0	0	0	0	0	0	0	0	0	0
170	175	9	0	0	0	0	0	0	0	0	0	0
175	180	10	0	0	0	0	0	0	0	0	0	0
180	185	11	0	0	0	0	0	0	0	0	0	0
185	190	12	0	0	0	0	0	0	0	0	0	0
190	195	12	0	0	0	0	0	0	0	0	0	0
195	200	13	0	0	0	0	0	0	0	0	0	0
200	205	14	0	0	0	0	0	0	0	0	0	0
205	210	15	0	0	0	0	0	0	0	0	0	0
210	215	15	0	0	0	0	0	0	0	0	0	0
215	220	16	0	0	0	0	0	0	0	0	0	0
220	225	17	0	0	0	0	0	0	0	0	0	0
225	230	18	0	0	0	0	0	0	0	0	0	0
230	235	18	1	0	0	0	0	0	0	0	0	0
235	240	19	2	0	0	0	0	0	0	0	0	0
240	245	20	2	0	0	0	0	0	0	0	0	0
245	250	21	3	0	0	0	0	0	0	0	0	0
250	260	22	4	0	0	0	0	0	0	0	0	0
260	270	23	6	0	0	0	0	0	0	0	0	0
270	280	25	7	0	0	0	0	0	0	0	0	0
280	290	26	9	0	0	0	0	0	0	0	0	0
290	300	28	10	0	0	0	0	0	0	0	0	0
300	310	29	12	0	0	0	0	0	0	0	0	0
310	320	31	13	0	0	0	0	0	0	0	0	0
320	330	32	15	0	0	0	0	0	0	0	0	0
330	340	34	16	0	0	0	0	0	0	0	0	0
340	350	35	18	0	0	0	0	0	0	0	0	0
350	360	37	19	2	0	0	0	0	0	0	0	0
360	370	38	21	3	0	0	0	0	0	0	0	0
370	380	40	22	5	0	0	0	0	0	0	0	0
380	390	41	24	6	0	0	0	0	0	0	0	0
390	400	43	25	8	0	0	0	0	0	0	0	0
400	410	44	27	9	0	0	0	0	0	0	0	0
410	420	46	28	11	0	0	0	0	0	0	0	0
420	430	47	30	12	0	0	0	0	0	0	0	0
430	440	49	31	14	0	0	0	0	0	0	0	0
440	450	50	33	15	0	0	0	0	0	0	0	0
450	460	52	34	17	0	0	0	0	0	0	0	0
460	470	53	36	18	1	0	0	0	0	0	0	0
470	480	55	37	20	2	0	0	0	0	0	0	0
480	490	56	39	21	4	0	0	0	0	0	0	0
490	500	58	40	23	5	0	0	0	0	0	0	0
500	520	60	42	25	7	0	0	0	0	0	0	0
520	540	63	45	28	10	0	0	0	0	0	0	0
540	560	66	48	31	13	0	0	0	0	0	0	0
560	580	69	51	34	16	0	0	0	0	0	0	0
580	600	72	54	37	19	2	0	0	0	0	0	0
600	620	75	57	40	22	5	0	0	0	0	0	0
620	640	78	60	43	25	8	0	0	0	0	0	0
640	660	81	63	46	28	11	0	0	0	0	0	0
660	680	84	66	49	31	14	0	0	0	0	0	0
680	700	87	69	52	34	17	0	0	0	0	0	0
700	720	90	72	55	37	20	2	0	0	0	0	0
720	740	93	75	58	40	23	5	0	0	0	0	0
740	760	96	78	61	43	26	8	0	0	0	0	0
760	780	99	81	64	46	29	11	0	0	0	0	0
780	800	102	84	67	49	32	14	0	0	0	0	0
800	820	105	87	70	52	35	17	0	0	0	0	0
820	840	108	90	73	55	38	20	3	0	0	0	0

Page 44

Payroll Registers

PAYROLL REGISTER for the Weekly Payroll Period Ended March 15, 2003

NO.	NAME	MARITAL STATUS	EXEMP.	EARNINGS REGULAR	OVERTIME	TOTAL	DEDUCTIONS FEDERAL INCOME TAX	FICA	MEDICARE	OTHER	TOTAL DEDUCTIONS	NET PAY AMOUNT
1	Andrea Baker	S	1	800 00		800 00	87 00	49 60	11 60		148 20	651 80
2	Samuel Craig	S	1	800 00		800 00	87 00	49 60	11 60		148 20	651 80
	Totals			1600 00		1600 00	174 00	99 20	23 20		296 40	1303 60

PAYROLL REGISTER for the Weekly Payroll Period Ended March 31, 2003

NO.	NAME	MARITAL STATUS	EXEMP.	EARNINGS REGULAR	OVERTIME	TOTAL	DEDUCTIONS FEDERAL INCOME TAX	FICA	MEDICARE	OTHER	TOTAL DEDUCTIONS	NET PAY AMOUNT
1	Andrea Baker	S	1	800 00		800 00	87 00	49 60	11 60		148 20	651 80
2	Samuel Craig	S	1	800 00		800 00	87 00	49 60	11 60		148 20	651 80
3	Seaton Lewis	S	0	200 00		200 00	14 00	12 40	2 90		29 30	170 70
	Totals			1800 00		1800 00	188 00	111 60	26 10		325 70	1474 30

Employer's Payroll Tax Summary

Payroll Tax Summary Sheet March 15, 20–   *Memo #5*

	Debit	*Credit*
Payroll Taxes Expense	$204.00	
FICA Tax Payable		$99.20
Medicare Tax Payable		$23.20
Unemployment Tax Payable – Federal		$12.80
Unemployment Tax Payable – State		$68.80

Payroll Tax Summary Sheet March 31, 20–   *Memo #12*

	Debit	*Credit*
Payroll Taxes Expense	$229.50	
FICA Tax Payable		$111.60
Medicare Tax Payable		$26.10
Unemployment Tax Payable – Federal		$14.40
Unemployment Tax Payable – State		$77.40

24

Olive Larson's Tours
Work Sheet
For the month ended March 31, 2003

ACCT. NO.	ACCOUNT NAME	TRIAL BALANCE DEBIT	TRIAL BALANCE CREDIT	ADJUSTMENTS DEBIT	ADJUSTMENTS CREDIT	INCOME STATEMENT DEBIT	INCOME STATEMENT CREDIT	BALANCE SHEET DEBIT	BALANCE SHEET CREDIT
110	Cash	14350 50						14350 50	
120	Petty Cash	300 00						300 00	
130	Supplies	3685 00			(a) 2505 00			1180 00	
140	Prepaid Insurance	5140 00			(b) 3110 00			2030 00	
150	Automobile	17950 00						17950 00	
160	Office Equipment	2695 00						2695 00	
210	A/P Office Supply		445 00						445 00
220	Employee Income Tax Payable		362 00						362 00
230	FICA Tax Payable		421 60						421 60
240	First City Bank		9800 00						9800 00
250	Medicare Tax Payable		98 60						98 60
260	Unemploy. Tax Payable - Federal		27 20						27 20
270	Unemploy. Tax Payable - State		141 20						141 20
310	Olive Larson, Capital		35000 00						35000 00
320	Olive Larson, Drawing	2550 00						2550 00	
330	Income Summary								
410	Tour Fees		21905 00				21905 00		
510	Advertising Expense	1118 50				1118 50			
520	Automobile Expense	1725 35				725 35 DK			
530	Insurance Expense			(b) 3110 00		3110 00			
540	Miscellaneous Expense	1715 75				1715 75			
550	Payroll Taxes Expense	433 50				433 50			
560	Rent Expense	1250 00				1250 00			
570	Salary Expense	3400 00				3400 00			
580	Supplies Expense			(a) 2505 00		2505 00			
590	Utilities Expense	1392 00				1392 00			
	Total	56706 60	56705 60	5615 00	5615 00	15650 10	21905 00	41055 50	34800 60
	Net Income					+ 6254 90			6254 90
						21905 00	21905 00	41055 50	41055 50

Income Statement

Larson's Tour
Income Statement
For the month ended March 31, 2005

Revenue:							
Tour Fees					21,905	00
Expenses:						
Advertising Expense	1118	50			
Automobile Expense	725	35			
Insurance Expense	3110	00			
Miscellaneous Expense	1715	75			
Payroll Expense	433	50			
Rent Expense	1250	00			
Salary Expense	3400	00			
Supplies Expense	2505	00			
Utilities Expense	1392	00			
Total Expense			15650	10	
Net Income			6254	90	

26

Statement of Owner's Equity

Olive Larson's Tour
Statement of Owner's Equity
FOR THE MONTH ENDED March 31, 2003

Capital, March 1, 2003			23500 00
Add: Net Income			6254 90
Total			29754 90
Less: WithDrawls			2550 00
Olive Larson's, Capital, March 31, 2003			27204 90
Capital, March 1, 2003			22000 00
Add: ADDITIONAL INVESTMENTS	1500 00		
Net Income	6254 90		
Net Increase In Capital			7754 90
Total			29754 90
Less: WithDrawls			2550 00
Olive Larson's, Capital, March 31, 2003			27204 90

Balance Sheet

Lassm's Tours
Balance Sheet
March 31, 2003

Assets				
Cash	14350	50		
Petty Cash	300	00		
Supplies	1180	00		
Prepaid Insurance	2030	00		
Automobile	17,950	00		
Office Equipment	2,695	00		
			38505	50
Liabilities				
A to Z Office Supply	445	00		
Employee Income Tax Payable	362	00		
FICA Tax Payable	421	60		
First City Bank	9800	00		
Medicare Tax Payable	98	60		
Unemployment Tax Payable - Federal	27	20		
Unemployment Tax Payable - State	146	20		
			11300	60
Owner's Equity				
Oliver Lassm Capital			27204	90
Total Liabilities + Owner's Equity			38505	50

Total → Assets

Total Liabilities

Post-Closing Trial Balance

Tammy's Toms
Trial balance
For the month ended March 31, 2003

ACCOUNT TITLE	ACCT. NO.	DEBIT		CREDIT	
Cash	110	14350	50		
Petty Cash	120	300	00		
Supplies	130	1180	00		
Prepaid Insurance	140	2030	00		
Automobile	150	17,950	00		
Office Equipment	160	2,695	00		
A to Z Office Supply	210			445	00
Employee Income Tax Payable	220			362	00
FICA Tax Payable	230			421	60
First City Bank	240			9800	00
Medicare Tax Payable	250			98	60
Unemployment Tax Payable – Federal	260			27	20
Unemployment Tax Payable – State	270			146	20
Olive Larson, Capital	310			27204	90
Olive Larson, Drawing	320	38505	50	38505	50
Income Summary	330				

GLOSSARY

Account – a record that summarizes all the characteristics of a single item of the equation.

Account Balance – the computed balance of an account after all debits and credits have been posted.

Account Format – a balance sheet format that lists the assets on the left and the liabilities and equity on the right, similar to the accounting equation.

Account Number – the number assigned to an account in the ledger.

Account Title – the name given to any account.

Accountant – a person responsible for interpreting financial data.

Adjusting Entries – entries made in the journal to adjust the ledger accounts so that they will contain the same balances as shown on the worksheet.

Adjustments – an adjustment is an amount that is added to or subtracted from an account balance to bring the balance up to date.

Asset – anything of value that is owned.

Assets/Expense Adjustment – a type of deferral adjustment that distributes the expense of consumed assets (such as supplies) over more than one fiscal period.

Balance Column Account – an account that has debit and credit columns for entering changes in the account and a column for entering the new account balance after each debit or credit is posted to the account.

Balance Sheet – a form that shows the financial position of a business on a specific date.

Basic Accounting Equation – a formula that illustrates the relationship between assets, liabilities and capital; Assets = Liabilities + Capital.

Beginning Balance Sheet – a balance sheet prepared on the day the business starts.

Book of Original Entry – any journal used in an accounting system.

Book of Secondary Entry – any ledger used in an accounting system.

Bookkeeper – a person responsible for recording business transactions.

Business Entity – the existence of a business as an artificial individual.

Business Transaction – business activity that causes changes in the value of assets, liabilities and capital.

Capital – the financial interest of the owner of a business; determined by subtracting total liabilities from the total assets. Also called Owner's Equity.

Chart of Accounts – a list of all accounts used by an entity indicating the identifying number, the account title and classification of each accounting equation item.

Chronological – in order by date.

Closing Entries – journal entries prepared at the end of a fiscal period to transfer the balances of revenue and expense accounts to the proprietor's Capital account.

Compound Entry – a journal entry that contains more than two accounts.

Consistent Reporting – the same accounting concepts are applied the same way for each accounting period for as long as the business operates.

Contra Account – an account that has a negative effect on a controlling account.

Corporation – an association of individuals united for a common purpose to use a common name and to change members without dissolving the association; a business chartered under state law and owned by stockholders.

Credit – refers to any entry made in the right-hand amount column of a general journal.

Creditor – anyone to whom a business owes money.

Debit – refers to any entry made in the left-hand amount column of a general journal.

Deferral Adjustments – adjustments to accounts that delay the recognition of the expenses or revenue until a fiscal period later than the one during which the cash was paid or the liability incurred.

Double-entry Accounting – each financial transaction has a double effect and is recorded so that the total of the debit amounts is always equal to the total of the credit amounts.

Drawing – an owner's withdrawal of cash from his business for personal use.

Employee Earnings Record – a form used to summarize payroll deductions and payments made to each individual employee.

Entry – a transaction recorded in journal.

Equities – the claims against the assets of a business.

Expenses – the cost of goods and services used in the operation of a business.

Federal Insurance Contribution Act (FICA) – a law requiring employers and employees to pay taxes to the federal government to support the Social Security programs; the term "FICA" is also used to refer to the taxes themselves.

Federal Unemployment Tax Act (FUTA) – a federal tax used for administration of state and federal unemployment programs.

File Maintenance – the procedure of arranging accounts in a general ledger, inserting and deleting accounts, and keeping records current.

Fiscal Period – the length of the accounting cycle for which a business summarizes and reports financial information.

General Ledger – contains all the accounts needed to prepare financial statements.

Gross Earnings – the total amount due each employee for the pay period before any payroll deductions; also referred to as gross pay.

Income – the difference between revenue from the sale of goods and services and the expenses that come from operating the business and making the sales.

Income Statement – a financial statement that reports the revenue, expenses and net income or net loss of a business for a specific period of time.

Income Summary Account – a temporary account whose balance is transferred to the permanent Capital account at the end of each accounting period.

Journal – a business form used for recording accounting information in chronological order with transactions analyzed in terms of the accounts to be debited and credited.

Journalizing – recording information in chronological order in the journal, using the source document as evidence of the business transaction.

Ledger – a group of accounts.

Liability – any amount that is owed.

Liquidity – ease of converting an item to cash.

Matching Expenses with Revenue – all revenue and expenses associated with a business activity are to be recorded in the same accounting period.

Merit Rating – a rating used to adjust an employer's state unemployment tax liability based upon a record of steady employment.

Net – the amount remaining after all deductions have been made.

Net Income – the difference between total revenue and total expenses when total revenue is greater than total expenses.

Net Loss – the difference between total revenue and total expenses when total expenses are greater than total revenue.

Opening an Account – writing the account title and number on the heading line of an account.

Opening Entry – the first entry made in a general journal that opens the accounts in a new set of books.

Owner's Equity (Capital) – the financial interest of the owner of a business; determined by subtracting total assets from the total liabilities.

Partnership – an association of two or more persons to carry on as co-owners of a business for profit.

Pay Period – a period covered by a salary payment.

Payroll – all salaries and wages paid to employees.

Payroll Deductions – required and voluntary deductions from gross earnings to determine net pay.

Payroll Register – an accounting form that summarizes payroll information for all employees during a specific pay period.

Permanent Accounts – accounts that accumulate financial information from one fiscal period to another; also known as real accounts.

Post-Closing Trial Balance – a trial balance completed to check the equality of the debits and credits in the general ledger accounts that remain open after the closing process has been completed.

Posting – the process of transferring the information from a journal entry to the ledger accounts.

Proprietor – the owner of a business.

Proving Cash – the process of determining whether the amount of cash, both on hand and in the bank, is the same amount that exists in the accounting records.

Quarterly – every three months; in a calendar year the quarters are January through March, April through June, July through September and October through December.

Report Format – the most common balance sheet format, with the asset section listed first, followed by the liability and equity sections. This is a two-column report similar to the income statement.

Revenue – the increase in owner's equity caused by income from the sale of goods and services.

Ruling – refers to drawing a line. A single line means the entries above are complete. A double line means the figures have been verified as correct.

Salary – a specified amount paid to an employee per month or per year.

Semimonthly – twice a month; refers to a pay period that usually falls on the 15th and the 31st the month.

Sole proprietorship – a business owned and managed by one person.

Source Document – a written or printed paper that provides evidence that a transaction occurred and gives the information needed to analyze the transaction; e.g., a purchase invoice, a check stub, a receipt, a memorandum, etc.

State Unemployment Tax – a tax imposed by a state to pay benefits to the unemployed.

Statement of Owner's Equity – the financial statement that reports the changes in capital that have occurred between the beginning and ending of a given fiscal period.

Transaction – an action that changes the value of the assets, liabilities and capital of a business entity.

T Account – an accounting device used to analyze business transactions.

Temporary Accounts – accounts (such as Revenue and Expenses) that gather data for one accounting period only; accounts used to compute net income for each accounting period.

Time and a Half – a term used to describe the rate a worker is paid for overtime. The overtime rate is the worker's regular hourly rate ("time") plus half his regular rate ("and a half").

Trial Balance – a proof (test) to show that the total debit balances in the ledger equal the total credit balances.

Wages – payment based on an hourly rate or a piecework basis.

Withholding Allowance – the number of persons legally supported by the taxpayer.

Working Papers – informal, informational papers provided by accountants to owners and managers.

Worksheet – a columnar accounting form used to summarize the general ledger information needed to prepare financial statements.

Temporary Accounts – accounts that accumulate financial information until it is transferred to the owner's Capital account; also known as nominal accounts.